BLACK HILLS

RENARD PRESS — PLAYSCRIPT III

BLACK HILLS: ORIGINAL READING AT PLEASANCE THEATRE IN 2019, DIRECTED BY TESS AGUS, MOVEMENT DIRECTION BY SEAN CROFT, PRODUCED BY MARK LINDOW. SCOTT PLAYED BY CHRISTOPHER HUNTER, JOANIE PLAYED BY MADELEINE DALY, CARRIE PLAYED BY MEL WOODBRIDGE AND DARRYL PLAYED BY MARK GRINDROD.

SPECIAL THANKS TO ANTHONY LAU AND JULES HAWORTH AT THE SOHO THEATRE WRITERS LAB.

BY THE SAME AUTHOR:

FRIDGE

PLAYSCRIPT I

9781913724238

IN THE MOSS

PLAYSCRIPT II

9781913724559

BLACK HILLS

EMMA ZADOW

RENARD PRESS

RENARD PRESS LTD

124 City Road
London EC1V 2NX
United Kingdom
info@renardpress.com
020 8050 2928

www.renardpress.com

Black Hills first published by Renard Press Ltd in 2022

Text © Emma Zadow, 2022
Cover design by Will Dady

Printed in the United Kingdom by Severn

ISBN: 978-1-913724-96-2

9 8 7 6 5 4 3 2 1

Renard Press is proud to be a climate positive publisher, removing more carbon from the air than we emit and planting a small forest. For more information see renardpress.com/eco.

Emma Zadow asserts her right to be identified as the author of this work in accordance with the Copyright, Designs and Patents Act 1988.

This is a work of fiction. Any resemblance to actual persons, living or dead, is purely coincidental.

All rights reserved. This publication may not be reproduced, stored in a retrieval system or transmitted, in any form or by any means – electronic, mechanical, photocopying, recording or otherwise – without the prior permission of the publisher.

Permission for producing this play may be applied for via the publisher, using the contact details above, or by emailing rights@renardpress.com.

CONTENTS

Black Hills	7
Scene One	11
Scene Two	18
Scene Three	29
Scene Four	31
Scene Five	40
Scene Six	43
Scene Seven	52
Scene Eight	55
Scene Nine	59
Acknowledgements	75

BLACK HILLS

CHARACTERS

CARRIE
Late forties, 1968.

SCOTT
Mid twenties, 1968 and 1973.

JOANIE
Early twenties, 1973.

DARRYL
Late forties, 1973.

The action takes place in the same space – a kitchen and diner. All actors remain on stage, unless specified, moving in and out of focus between 1968 and 1973. There is a small bar counter stage left, and a table and four chairs stage right. A door upstage centre serves both 1968 and 1973. There is a second entrance downstage left. The kitchen and diner are not two separate places, but rather exist together, overlapping with each other on stage. A collage.

NOTES
A colour indicates a shift in light and character.

SCENE ONE

A kitchen on the east coast of America, 1968. There are clothes, make-up, a few books and bottles strewn across the floor. The remnants of a party. Radio tuning sound hisses. 'Chirpy Chirpy Cheep Cheep' by Middle of the Road echoes. Blue light floods the space. CARRIE *nurses a martini, and is collapsed on the floor, cross-legged. She wears a peignoir gown and dress set in a faded peach or coral pastel colour. She lights a cigarette. Inhales. Exhales with relief. She crawls with her cigarette to a cereal box on the floor. She looks inside. She pours the cereal into her hand and eats a few bits dry. Unsatisfied, she reaches for the nearest bottle. It is only a third full. She uncaps it. She pours it into the cereal box. She watches the last drips fall from the bottle into the box. The cereal crackles and pops. Silence. She looks around for a spoon. Silence.*)

SCOTT (*offstage*): Mom?!

(*White.* CARRIE *panics. She stubs out her cigarette. In the gloom, she puts on a pair of sunglasses.*)

I'm not staying long, but I gotta pick up my bike…

(SCOTT *enters. He is smartly dressed. Clean. He looks around at the space.*)

Mom—
CARRIE: Oh, um, yes, I suppose. It is a little… isn't it?
SCOTT: You're lucky Joanie's at softball practice.
CARRIE: Softball practice. (*She giggles.*) I forget what sports they come up with these days.

(*Pause.*)

SCOTT: What's that noise?
CARRIE: I don't hear anything.
SCOTT: That… that popping.
CARRIE: Crackle. It's a crackle. Not a pop.
SCOTT: What's that *crackle*, then?
CARRIE: Breakfast.
SCOTT: It's four. (*Pause.*) In the afternoon.

(CARRIE *puts her hand in the cereal box and eats the wet cereal loudly.*)

SCOTT: Those are Joanie's.

CARRIE: I paid for them!
SCOTT: *Dad* paid for them.
CARRIE: I bought them!
SCOTT: Why do you do this?
CARRIE: There wasn't any milk.

(*Pause.* SCOTT *inspects the room.*)

SCENE ONE

SCOTT: We'll have to clean all this up.
CARRIE (*cradling her glass*): Oh come on, a clean house can only mean one thing.
SCOTT (*imitating her*): A happy Scott?
CARRIE: Boring people. Only boring people have clean homes.

(*Pause.*)

SCOTT: You know what Dad's like when he knows they've been here. And *I* don't want that, and *you* don't want that, and *we* don't want Joanie to know anything about it.
CARRIE: I like having friends around, and they are very *interesting* people, with ideas you'd like, I think. Very *cultured*. We just like talking and drinking together… like a book club. A book club with personalities.
SCOTT: I believed that at first, when it *was* a book club, but now… It's not that I don't like them, it's only… they don't really belong here, do they? I mean, they're from the… the Village – they just… well… you know.
CARRIE: They're what, from big bad New York City?
SCOTT: You know.
CARRIE: I know a lot about a lot. But please remind me. I'm curious.

(*Pause.*)

Oh, do spit it out!
SCOTT: They… they don't mix with green grass and cinnamon toasts, all right?
CARRIE: Do you have a problem with creative people, Scott?

SCOTT: No, I don't. They're… wonderful people, they are. But they don't belong here.
CARRIE: Why not?
SCOTT: They're happy.
CARRIE: But we're happy, aren't we?

(*Pause.* SCOTT *begins to fold the clothes up into a neat pile upstage.*)

Oh, aren't we superb liars?! I always thought you should have trodden the boards. I could always call my old agent and pull a few strings. So easily done these days!
SCOTT: I don't think so.
CARRIE: It would be such a shame to put that talent to waste.
SCOTT: I have other talents.
CARRIE: You're… patient.
SCOTT: Patience isn't a talent. I do have other virtues.
CARRIE: But none as fun as lying to people who love you. Who love you because of it, and who come back to see the same show again and again. There's no greater thrill than telling a lie and getting away with it.
SCOTT: Oh, I think…

(*He stops himself. He notices a stain in the middle of the space. He starts to scrub the floor with a cloth from his pocket.*)

CARRIE: Go on. You were about to—
SCOTT: It really doesn't matter.
CARRIE: Come on.
SCOTT: I said it doesn't matter. Just an idea.
CARRIE: Try explaining that one to your father.

SCENE ONE

(SCOTT *rolls up his sleeves and continues to scrub. He wipes his forehead.* CARRIE *studies him from the side.*)

You know, you've got the perfect profile for Arthur Miller. All that frowning. And strong knees, too. His men always end up on their knees. If you're on your knees in a Miller, you know you're going to get the best lines.

(*She inspects him from the other side, like a racehorse.*)

Perfect.
SCOTT: I hate the theatre. It's just a bunch of people saying words they don't mean to people who don't know how to feel in their own lives, so they come to see other people do it for them.
CARRIE: Meow! And such self-hatred – I love it! You're a born actor, Scottie!
SCOTT: I said I hated the theatre.
CARRIE: Did you?
SCOTT: It's still filthy.

(*They look at each other. He goes back to the stain on the floor and begins to scrub again.*)

CARRIE (*wounded*): Are you telling me off?
SCOTT: No.

(*He scrubs faster.*)

CARRIE: You're upset with me.

SCOTT: No.
CARRIE: You're disappointed in me.
SCOTT: No.
CARRIE: You're angry with me.

(SCOTT *scrubs harder.*)

SCOTT: No. I'm *not* angry. I'm not. I'm not angry with you.
CARRIE: Then what, darling?

(*Pause.*)

SCOTT: There. (*He wipes his forehead again.*) It's clean now. Nothing to worry about.
CARRIE: I'll help.
SCOTT: It's done now.

(*Slight pause.*)

CARRIE: You make it sound so simple – why can't you be the parent and I be the child? Oh, Scottie, why can't I have fun?
SCOTT: It's—
CARRIE: Confusing?

(*She smiles and sips from her glass.*)

SCOTT: You're my Mom – you're not supposed to have fun now. God, other moms pick their kids up from school; you drive around aimlessly for hours. Other moms make dinner. Mine? She makes martinis.

CARRIE: You say that like it's a bad thing. When you live in the 'burbs you'll understand.

SCOTT: I already do!

CARRIE: It's not the same thing! (*Pause. She stares down into her glass.*) It's empty.

SCOTT: I'm not saying you need to be like every mom… but, well… can't you just be a *little* like them?

CARRIE: No.

SCOTT: Oh.

CARRIE: I'm glad we sorted that out, darling.

(CARRIE *kisses* SCOTT *on the cheek and goes off in search of another bottle.*)

SCENE TWO

The Black Hills in South Dakota, 1973. A roadside diner in the middle of the night. Door slams. CARRIE *finds a bottle a third-full again. She pours the bottle into her glass and leans against the wall absently. A radio tuning sound.* JOANIE *enters. She is more ragged in appearance, and wears a loud men's coat of the time and carries a heavy suitcase. She runs furiously through the diner, across the space, to the upstage door.*

JOANIE: Hey!

(JOANIE *pushes past* SCOTT. *She throws the suitcase down by the upstage door.*)

> What did you say? We're not done here! You said you'd take us as far as Casper! Idiots!

(*She throws her head back and spits out of the door. She gestures to* SCOTT *to join her. He moves behind her.*)

> Yeah, there's plenty more of that comin' to you! (*Aside to* SCOTT.) Nice hook back there. Right on the chin… You don't get to say that about Scott! FUCKERS!

SCOTT: Joanie—
JOANIE: Yeah! You keep driving! We don't need you, anyway! And for the record, Scott *hates* Billy Joel!
SCOTT: Joanie!
JOANIE: What?
SCOTT: That's enough.

(JOANIE *spits out of the door again, raising her arms in contempt.* SCOTT *leans past her to look out of the door.*)

SCOTT: They're coming back!

(*They look at each other. Pause.*)

JOANIE: Don't you say a word.

(*Bright white.* DARRYL *enters through the upstage diner door between them. He is brawny and wears an earth-stained jacket. He throws* SCOTT *and* JOANIE *on to the table.*)

SCOTT: Hey, hey, look, I'm sorry about that... we're... you... she... I... I'm really sorry about the Billy Joel thing.
DARRYL: What the hell do you think you were trying to prove? You can't play around here! They're tense enough as it is.
SCOTT: I thought—
DARRYL: Does this look like the Harvard dining hall, kid? Nothing but Black Hills here, Kennedy Boy.
SCOTT: Great. Just great.

DARRYL: What did you think they were going to do? Spitting at the boys like that on *their* turf. Besides, what're you doing out here anyway? Not exactly a place for… (*looking* SCOTT *up and down*) a Kennedy, if you know what I mean. Too empty.
SCOTT: I'm not a—
JOANIE: We're passing through.
DARRYL: Good. Guessing no wheels?
SCOTT: Thanks to her, yeah.
DARRYL: They still there?

(SCOTT *and* JOANIE *move to see.*)

Don't look.
JOANIE: Uh, yeah.
DARRYL: I said don't look. Where are you heading?
SCOTT: Oregon. Reed.
DARRYL: Right.
JOANIE: It's a college.
DARRYL: Well, you'd be a fool to stay out east. Falling apart, they say. Look, I'm going to the bar. See what I can do. Do *not* leave this table. Now, give me an order to walk with.

(SCOTT *is speechless.*)

You're not helping me here.
JOANIE: How about a beer?
DARRYL: You old enough for that, darlin'?
JOANIE: Fine. A cola then.
DARRYL (*he sings teasingly*): I'd like to buy the gal a Coke…

SCENE TWO

JOANIE: Err… (*She sings:*) What I want today is the real thing…

DARRYL (*laughing*): That's it. Good. Good. *She's* got the right idea.

(DARRYL *goes to the bar. He takes* CARRIE's *glass from her. He begins to clean it.*)

JOANIE: You didn't have to do that. Now we're just stranded out here, thanks to you.

SCOTT: Me?

JOANIE: Yeah, you.

SCOTT: Of course it's my fault. It's always my fault.

JOANIE: You're not on trial.

SCOTT: I'm just trying to look out for you.

JOANIE: Thanks.

(*Pause.*)

SCOTT: It's cool. What I'm here for, right? You. Even if you do pick my fights for me. For the record, you started it.

(JOANIE *rolls her eyes.*)

Anyway, we've got to be our own mom and dad now.

JOANIE: Well, I'm not being the mom.

SCOTT: Oh, we're doing that are we? OK, you're Mom.

JOANIE: Why do I have to be the mom?

SCOTT: Because you don't want to be.

JOANIE: And you should be the dad because you don't want to be.

SCOTT: But... you're the girl, you should be the mom.

JOANIE: Excuse me? We need to get you to Reed fast. Just because I'm a girl doesn't mean I'm the mom – not our mom, anyway.

SCOTT: You're saying you're calling Dad?

JOANIE: Uh... yeah. Let's see why, shall we? He didn't think 'Is this all?' So yeah, I'm calling dibs on the dad.

SCOTT: I call neither.

JOANIE: I didn't know that was an option.

SCOTT: Trick question.

JOANIE: Cheater.

SCOTT: Loser.

(*Pause.*)

JOANIE: Guess I'm good at making quick decisions. (*Pause.*) Still working on this one, though.

SCOTT: You seemed pretty quick back there...

JOANIE: So did you!

SCOTT: And you with the quick fists!

JOANIE: I got the last one in!

SCOTT: You started it with them!

JOANIE: You didn't hear what they said.

SCOTT: What? What did they say?

JOANIE: It was about you... Use your imagination. (*Pause.*) But we know where we're going.

SCOTT: Oregon.

JOANIE: That's right. You got in, Scott!

SCOTT: Reed College! Oregon! West Coast! Right where we need to be. It's going to change everything, Joanie. I promise. And we'll be making it. The doors are wide open for us! It's not over out there.

JOANIE: Where the change is really happening.

SCOTT: A fresh start, sis!

JOANIE: A chance is what we got out there!

SCOTT: We're not stopping!

JOANIE: No one's gonna touch us. Ever.

SCOTT: That's right. Oh boy, that's right.

JOANIE: You OK?

SCOTT: Yeah, yeah. Just... sitting tight in these hills where the roads drive those men, I can't—

JOANIE: They're all driving the roads now. The... scum and scuttlers... House... to... House... to... House... Don't make no difference.

SCOTT: Spines scuttling up ceilings.

JOANIE: Spines scuttling up ceilings.

(*Pause.* JOANIE *turns back to* SCOTT *like a child.*)

Wake up to a note from Mom on the fridge. Find the Spaghetti Os.

JOANIE: Can opener?

SCOTT: Stab it with a fork.

JOANIE: Suck out the tomato cheese juice.

SCOTT: Don't need a straw.

JOANIE: Drain it dry.

SCOTT: Spit out the Os.

JOANIE: You always beat me at that.

(CARRIE *giggles at a memory and slumps to the floor.*)

SCOTT: Wipe your mouth.
JOANIE: Juice on my sleeve.
SCOTT: Forget my homework.
JOANIE: Blame the dog we don't have!
SCOTT: Blame you!
JOANIE: Hand-me-down shirt.
SCOTT: You stole it! And you liked it!
JOANIE: Get in trouble.
SCOTT: Picked on.
JOANIE: Kicked on.
ALL: 'Such a bad influence.'
SCOTT: 'I don't know what she feeds them!'
JOANIE: Rip the note off the fridge.
SCOTT: Their handwriting.
JOANIE: Keep it in your pocket all day.

(JOANIE *takes a letter from her pocket. She holds in front of* SCOTT. *Pause.*)

SCOTT: Hide it so no one will see.

(*Pause.* SCOTT *touches the corner of the letter and pushes it back to* JOANIE. *She puts it back in her pocket.* SCOTT *looks out the door again. They recover.*)

Hey, I don't think I can see them out there any more.
JOANIE: Gone?
SCOTT: Maybe.
JOANIE: I think we should wait until he comes back.

SCOTT: We don't know if he will.

JOANIE: I don't want to go out there alone.

SCOTT: And you're not going to. He'll come back with a ride out of here. Seems like he cares. Enough. Further and further apart, I'm finding.

JOANIE: What are?

(DARRYL *finishes cleaning* CARRIE*'s glass and places it on the bar.*)

SCOTT: People giving a damn.

JOANIE: We've got this far.

SCOTT: Well, we aren't getting any further with your temper.

JOANIE: My temper?

SCOTT: Yes, you can't... you... can't... be angry all the time.

JOANIE: I am *not* angry all the time!

SCOTT: You know what I mean.

JOANIE: You want to do this? Now? You really want to do this?

SCOTT: Hey, we've got over twenty-four hours on the road to go before Reed – I was going to bring it up back East, but well—

JOANIE: What's this about?

SCOTT: Don't take this the wrong way.

JOANIE: Don't say the wrong thing.

SCOTT: All right. First there was that guy you took a swing at—

JOANIE: An accident. And it was high school. I was clumsy.

SCOTT: Then there was that jock at the game—

JOANIE: He was a jerk and a perv.

SCOTT: Then the guy in the line at Wendy's—

JOANIE: He looked at me funny. You saw him!
SCOTT: Our mailman!
JOANIE: So?
SCOTT: You tried to beat up the mailman.

(*Pause.*)

It's got to stop.
JOANIE: And this is you suddenly wanting to 'save me from myself'? Are you going to 'sort me out', big brother? Is this an *in-ter-ven-tion*?
SCOTT: This isn't me doing PSYCH 101 on you.

(*Pause.* JOANIE *sticks her tongue out at* SCOTT, *turning from him.*)

(*Struggling:*) We're not kids any more. It was a long time ago. And you've got to stop with this 'poor me' thing you've got going on.
JOANIE: Don't try and—
SCOTT: Listen!
JOANIE: Look at you trying to take charge.

(CARRIE *tries to get up, but falls back down with a slam.*)

SCOTT: I'm not a replacement for Dad, and you can't expect to go find one out there or in me.
JOANIE: Damn. You've found me out, Doctor Scott.
SCOTT: Wow. You really are—
JOANIE: You think I'm playing victim? You think I'm Daddy's little girl, lost out here, stranded with you?

I'm not some little girl, I'm right where I'm supposed to be.

SCOTT: In the middle of nowhere?

JOANIE: I like being lost. You should try it.

(*Pause.*)

We're invincible, us two. That's the one thing I learnt from Mom. If you want to go your own way, you gotta be alone in the world. That's why we have each other.

SCOTT: Joanie, you can't pick and choose what you want to take from the past. You're being unrealistic.

JOANIE: And you're being idealistic. The truth is we're stuck in these Black Hills, waiting on a ride to Oregon. That may sound unrealistic to you, but it's the truth.

SCOTT: I know. All I'm saying is you can't just blame Mom for everything that happened.

JOANIE: She made a choice.

SCOTT: And?

JOANIE: She didn't choose us!

(*Pause.*)

Now… we are going to Reed College. And we are going to be a part of something better. Something different… Something that's not *them*. Something that's not *old*. She left… Get over it. She did.

SCOTT: Joanie?

JOANIE: Yeah?

SCOTT: I need to make a call. There's a phone out back.
   (*He storms past her.*)
JOANIE (*grabbing his arm*): Stay.
SCOTT: Fine.
JOANIE: I love you, by the way.

(*They look at each other.* SCOTT *shrugs her off his arm.* JOANIE *retreats from him and folds her arms.*)

SCENE THREE

CARRIE *looks down at the scrubbed floor.*

CARRIE: Aw! That's so sweet. I don't know what I'd do without you!

(*She crawls back to the cereal box again and pours another bottle into it.*)

SCOTT: Don't you think you've had enough?
CARRIE (*coughing*): Are you calling me fat?!
SCOTT: No, no, no. I... I think you've had enough to *drink*, Mom.
CARRIE: Oh! You are funny! (*She laughs ecstatically.*)
SCOTT: Shhh...
CARRIE (*staggering up to standing*): Oh, I'm terribly sorry, Mrs Johnson, to have disturbed your ladies' bridge. It's just, I was having an epiphany about... and we'd run out of Vermouth, damn it!
SCOTT: Shhh... please—
CARRIE: I mean, what will Mrs Adams think of Mrs Connors now?!
SCOTT: STOP IT!

(CARRIE *stops. Silence.*)

CARRIE: Don't you ever tell me to shut up… I'm your mother. (*She staggers.*) I'm your goddamn mother… And I don't want to see you fight like that with your sister, you hear me? One day you're going to need each other. I'm not going to be here for ever.

(SCOTT *looks over to* JOANIE.)

Are you listening to me?
SCOTT: Yes.
CARRIE: Thank you. I'm trying to say… what a mom would.
SCOTT: You're doing fine.

SCENE FOUR

DARRYL *returns*.

DARRYL: So, I found a guy who's out by the tanks, but we gotta see if he'll take care of you all right. Got talkin' and he's been scouted for the As! Oakland Athletics! Can you believe that?

JOANIE: The As? That's the major leagues!

DARRYL: That's what he said. And from here! They're all going crazy for him.

JOANIE: Wow.

SCOTT: So where is he now?

DARRYL: He's gotta do a few errands before he heads out, but he'll be back soon. Filling the tank and all that. He's got a girl somewhere he needs to pick up too. You know.

SCOTT: We still have to wait, then?

DARRYL: Well, yeah, but it's a ride.

JOANIE: He can't be that bad. We're getting a lift with a major-league player!

DARRYL: Guessing you're a fan.

SCOTT: She's a pro.

JOANIE: Nah!

SCOTT: Oh yeah! Top. The best. The best of the best.
JOANIE: I was. But it was only Little League.
SCOTT: Well, you were little.

(JOANIE *mimes throwing and catching a softball in the air.*)

But you really were up there!
DARRYL: Pitching, I see?
JOANIE: Yeah.

(*She throws the imaginary ball up in the air again.*)

DARRYL: Baseball, eh?
JOANIE: Softball.
DARRYL: What's the difference?
JOANIE: Well, first you've got... well...

(*She rushes excitedly to arrange the chairs as the four bases and takes her coat off for the backstop. She picks up one of* CARRIE*'s bottles, which acts as a bat.*)

DARRYL: Is it that big too?
SCOTT: You wish!

(*Pause.* JOANIE *and* DARRYL *exchange awkward looks.*)

So, come on, coach, tell us.
JOANIE: OK. First, bases are the same, right? (*She points.*) One. Two. Three. Four. But the pitching area here (*she indicates somewhere in the middle of the chairs*) is much closer to the batter, see? Then you've got your pitcher.

SCENE FOUR

> The pitcher in baseball throws the ball *overarm* and a pitcher in softball throws the ball *underarm*. Like this. (*She demonstrates.*) We don't have a mound either. It's all about the throw. The acrobatics. The grace. The... reading your opponent. Got it?

DARRYL: I played football in high school.

JOANIE: Right... I need you (*points at* SCOTT) here. And you (*points at* DARRYL) here. You're gonna pitch to me. Can you do that?

(DARRYL *stands still and looks at* SCOTT. SCOTT *moves behind* DARRYL *as the catcher.*)

SCOTT: Don't look at me. She knows I can't.
JOANIE: I know you can't!
SCOTT: Hey!
JOANIE: It's easy.

(*She demonstrates a slow basic underarm pitch.* DARRYL *copies her.*)

> And then...

(*She demonstrates a slow screwball pitch.* DARRYL *copies her again.* JOANIE *then performs a screwball pitch at full speed. She smiles.* DARRYL *does not copy her.* SCOTT *laughs under his breath. She does it again, but even faster.*)

DARRYL: I think I'll play outfield for this.
SCOTT: Oh no, he can't get out of it! That's not fair!
JOANIE: Scott, you're up.

33

(SCOTT *walks up to pitch.* DARRYL *goes outfield, somewhere past the chairs, closer to the bar.*)

> Now, you've seen me play before, all those games? Just do what I do. Did. Just worse.

SCOTT (*flatly*): I don't like you when you play sports.
JOANIE: It's all about the swing.

(CARRIE *takes a large swig from her glass. It's empty. She searches for another bottle nearby.*)

CARRIE (*to the bottle she finds*): What's your secret?

(JOANIE *spits on either side of the bottle she's using as a bat and taps it twice on the back of each of her heels.*)

DARRYL: Is that really—
JOANIE: It's only on the outside.
DARRYL: Uhuh.
CARRIE: I've got a humdinger of one.

(CARRIE *crawls over behind where* JOANIE *is batting and slumps to the floor.*)

JOANIE: That's my secret to the best hit. Every time. Worked that time against the Cubs!
SCOTT: I was there! I remember that game.
JOANIE: That was a pretty sweet hit. Don't just stand there – you've got two feet, haven't you?
DARRYL: Thanks for reminding me. I'm great right here. (*He leans on the bar.*)

SCENE FOUR

JOANIE: Come on then. On your toes. This one is going to go around the stars and back. Are you watching? You ready? On your toes?

SCOTT: I'm on my toes!

JOANIE: I know you are – I was asking your team mate!

DARRYL: Darryl.

JOANIE: Good. You ready for me, Darryl?

DARRYL: Sure am.

SCOTT: The world is.

JOANIE: Come on, then!

(SCOTT *pretends to do the tricks he's seen* JOANIE *perform with the imaginary ball between his hands, throwing it up in the air.* SCOTT *is poised, ready to do a screwball pitch.* CARRIE *slides her head into her hands. Her fingers spread wide, running through her hair behind* JOANIE, *like a catcher.* JOANIE *and* DARRYL *stare at* SCOTT, *who is pretending to do tricks.*)

JOANIE: You've dropped it.

SCOTT: No I haven't.

JOANIE: Yes you have.

SCOTT: No I haven't, it's right here. (*He makes as though waving a ball at her.*) You blind or something?

(*Pause.*)

DARRYL: It's over here.

SCOTT: No it's not.

(DARRYL *picks an imaginary ball from the bar.*)

DARRYL: Oh, would you look at that, so it is. (*He throws it between his hands slowly.*)
SCOTT: I thought you said you've never played?
DARRYL: I guess I forgot.
SCOTT: Dirty play. And stunts like that before the first swing.
JOANIE: Now we're really in the leagues.

(DARRYL *throws it fast and hard to* SCOTT. SCOTT *reaches to catch it and swings around with the force of it. They exchange a look.*)

Scott, you ready?
SCOTT: Yep. You?
JOANIE: Come on, hit me with your best shot, big brother!

(SCOTT *pitches.* JOANIE *swings the bottle. There is a gunshot outside. Red. Dogs howl. Engines rev. Voices scream in revelry.* CARRIE *falls to the floor hard.* SCOTT *and* JOANIE *duck at the same time, their hands over their heads.* DARRYL *stands silent. Unmoving. Blank. He sees something out of the corner of his eye. White. Something passes through him.*)

DARRYL (*clapping his hands suddenly with glee, standing*): And you're outta there!

(*He brandishes the ball triumphantly.* SCOTT *and* JOANIE *peer up at him from the floor.*)

DARRYL: That'll be the Rez boys! (*Aside to* JOANIE:) I can tell you used to be good, kid.
JOANIE: The best.
DARRYL: Your folks teach you that?

SCENE FOUR

(JOANIE *rises and glares at him.* SCOTT *follows her and holds her hand firmly.*)

Let's see what we can do about that ride.

(DARRYL *moves to exit.*)

SCOTT: What the hell was that?
DARRYL: Nothin'. Gotta love those boys off the reservation!
JOANIE: You mean—
DARRYL: Yeah. You forgettin' you're in South Dakota, honey?
SCOTT: We didn't know. That's all.
DARRYL: You know that all-important life experience those colleges are after? You just found it.
SCOTT: I already got in.
DARRYL: Well, class has started, boy. And you're learning. Right here in the Black Hills.
SCOTT: Is that important to you?
DARRYL: Hey, I think we're going to get a campaign speech from the Man of the *People*, off to change the world!
SCOTT: What I mean is, is that where you're from?

(DARRYL *approaches* SCOTT. SCOTT *stands his ground. They are face to face.*)

DARRYL: Do you care?
SCOTT: Not really.
DARRYL: Then why ask?
SCOTT: I'm trying to improve my people skills.

37

(*Pause.* DARRYL *laughs again and moves away from* SCOTT.)

It's going to be different, Darryl.
DARRYL (*turning back*): Sure they are, kid. Sure they are.

(*He picks up the bottle* JOANIE *swung with. He walks slowly to the bar and puts the bottle down. He takes a pack of cigarettes and a lighter from his jacket. He hunches over the bar and throws the cigarette packet and lighter next to him on the counter. Silence.*)

CARRIE: Where did you go?
SCOTT: Joanie.

(*He tries to look* JOANIE *in the eye, but she looks away.*)

Joanie?
CARRIE: Scott?

(JOANIE *ignores* SCOTT *and moves to put the chairs back around the table.* SCOTT *helps her. They sit at the table.*)

SCOTT: Listen. Mom. Dad. (*Pause.*) No one gets here without both. Remember that.
JOANIE (*swinging her coat back on*): She made her choice. So did he. (*Pause. She rises.*) We've gotta make ours now.
SCOTT (*rising*): You are not going out there alone.
CARRIE: Look at me when I'm talking to you.
JOANIE: OK.

(SCOTT *stands over her. She leans her head towards him. Her arms go around him.*)

SCENE FOUR

SCOTT: OK?
JOANIE: OK.
SCOTT: I gotta make that call. Wait here. I won't be long.

(SCOTT *turns to exit.* JOANIE *watches him leave her.* *He trips over* CARRIE.)

SCENE FIVE

CARRIE: You look just like your father standing like that.
SCOTT: Oh.

(SCOTT *changes his position quickly.*)

CARRIE: Almost a man, Scottie, aren't you?
SCOTT: I don't know what you mean.

(CARRIE *looks at* SCOTT.)

   What?
CARRIE: Oh, nothing.

(*Pause.*)

SCOTT: You know, you should come to a game some time.
CARRIE: Oh yeah? How's she doing with it? I think I'd love baseball – all that throwing and catching and… running in circles.
SCOTT: It's a square. And it's softball.
CARRIE: Basically the same thing, right?

SCENE FIVE

SCOTT: Well, no—

CARRIE: Oh, I don't care about the details! Tell me what she's like – I bet she's a star!

SCOTT: She made the first team. Coach says she's got a great arm. She could make pitcher by the end of the year if she works hard enough at it. She really could do it, too, with the right coaching and support.

CARRIE: Who told you that?

SCOTT: Her coach.

CARRIE: Why didn't I know about it?

SCOTT: He told Dad. And Dad told me.

CARRIE: Right.

(CARRIE *gets up and moves to the bar. She picks up a glass and* DARRYL *fills it.*)

I don't know about all that sort of thing, anyway. Wasted on me, I'm afraid.

SCOTT: She's really good.

CARRIE: That's great. (*She drinks.*)

SCOTT: Maybe you could come to a game?

CARRIE: I already did that, darling, remember?

SCOTT: That was a year ago.

CARRIE: Yes?

(JOANIE *takes out the letter again from her pocket. She caresses the corners.* DARRYL *watches her.*)

SCOTT: It could be good for her to see you in the crowd again. You know, her mom being there might give her a bit of oomph on the field. The coach will be there, too. You could talk to him then.

CARRIE: Let me put it this way, sweetie: if I was in a play, you'd come and support me in the audience, right? And I'd be happy you came – I'd be thrilled, over the moon, in fact – and then you'd meet the director to hear all the funny stories from behind the scenes, and you'd tell me I was the best of them all. You'd say you loved me in the part. That I 'stood out from the rest'. But you wouldn't come back again, would you? Because it's the same show the second night, and the night after that and the night after that. Gosh, I remember being in a god-awful off-Broadway musical – oh, the choreography! And I wouldn't put you through that every night just so you could support me. That wouldn't be fair on you. You'd hate that. I'd be punishing you. You wouldn't want that, would you?

SCOTT: It's a completely different game every time, Mom.

CARRIE: From what I know, it's the same moves every time.

SCOTT: They play against different teams!

CARRIE: They use the same ball!

(*Pause.*)

SCOTT: Well, you might want to come again, to, you know, 'support', anyway. Just a suggestion. Don't feel pressured.

CARRIE: Your Dad can go. He knows the game better than me.

(CARRIE *turns away from* SCOTT.)

SCENE SIX

DARRYL *returns to the table with* JOANIE*'s cola.* JOANIE *hides the letter.*

DARRYL: This guy's cool, though. He'll take you as far as Redding. Like I said, tense. (*He looks around for* SCOTT.) I thought I told you to stay put? Your brother's gone.

JOANIE: He's out back.

(JOANIE *fumbles the letter again in her pocket.* CARRIE *gets up, giggling, and begins to dance by herself. She remembers a tune in her head. A sensual early jazz song can be heard, such as 'Shangri-La' by Robert Maxwell. She eggs* SCOTT *on to join her. He laughs and flatly refuses. He watches her.*)

DARRYL: How long's he going to be? Cos this ride won't wait for ever. The guy's on his way out of here, and I'd hate to see you two parted on the road.

JOANIE: I hope you don't mind if I... (*Takes a stick of gum from her pocket.*)

CARRIE: Look at me, Scott!

JOANIE: I get all fidgety in these situations. Sorry... It's peach if you want some?

(*Pause.*)

DARRYL: You got more to you than you let on, kid.
JOANIE: Aw, you'll make me ruin my make-up.
DARRYL: Don't bullshit me. You're pretty, and not many people look past pretty.
JOANIE: Pretty, huh?
DARRYL: Yeah. Why not?
JOANIE: Pretty gets you in trouble.
DARRYL: I wouldn't know.

(*Pause.*)

CARRIE: Oh! It used to be so very beautiful!
JOANIE: Don't look at me like that! (*She rises.*)
DARRYL: You've got an old man's temper in you, you know that?

(JOANIE *stares at him. She crosses her arms.*)

I've just got an eye for the troubled.
JOANIE: And the pretty.
DARRYL: Careful.

(*The lights flicker violently. Blue. White. Red. The radio tuning noise can be heard again.*)

No! No! No!

SCENE SIX

JOANIE: Are you all right?

(CARRIE *dances faster, giggling, and tries to get* SCOTT *to dance with her. She reaches to put his arm around her waist. He resists.* DARRYL *clenches his fists.*)

DARRYL: NO. STOP. MAKE. IT. STOP.

(*Darkness.* DARRYL *falls to the ground. His head is in his hands, and he's rocking, shaking, terrified, like an animal. He fits.* CARRIE *continues to dance alone in ecstasy. Her sunglasses fall off her head and on to the floor.* JOANIE *runs to* DARRYL. *The radio tuning sound is cut; 'Shangri-La' stops playing.*)

JOANIE: The power must have gone out.
DARRYL: I can't see anything! I can't see!
JOANIE: How do I make it stop?!
DARRYL: I can't see them.

(*Blue. Lights flicker again. Blue.*)

They're coming.

(JOANIE *pulls his hands away from his face. She clasps his wrists.*)

JOANIE: It's all right! You're all right – there's no one here to hurt you.
DARRYL: I can't see them. But they can see us.

(SCOTT *rises suddenly. The radio tuning sounds again, louder.*)

Incoming! Charlie's coming back for more! What are you doing, boy?

(SCOTT *grabs* CARRIE *and stops her dancing.*)

Run! Run, you poor bastard!

(SCOTT *pushes* CARRIE *into a chair and retreats to the other side of the room. He can't look at her.* DARRYL *pants harder, still rocking.*)

JOANIE: Breathe. Breathe with me. No one's going to hurt us. Breathe. OK? One… two… three… Count with me.

(JOANIE *and* DARRYL *count together.*)

DARRYL: I can't see!

(DARRYL *shakes violently again. He pulls away from* JOANIE.)

JOANIE: Hey. Hey.

(*The lights flicker. Blue.* DARRYL *shivers.* JOANIE *moves to hold his wrists again. He grabs hers before she can.*)

DARRYL: They're here.

(*He locks eyes with her.*)

JOANIE: Only I can see you.

(DARRYL *whimpers.*)

SCENE SIX

Listen. You got a wife?
DARRYL: I don't know!
JOANIE: OK, OK. You got family – kids?
DARRYL: Yeah—
JOANIE: How many?
DARRYL: One... a daughter.
JOANIE: What's her name?
DARRYL: Ruth.

(*Lights flicker. Red. Radio tuning is heard even louder. Darkness.* DARRYL *shivers violently. Lights flicker throughout now.*)

JOANIE: Look at me. Your daughter – remember, Ruth – how old is she?
DARRYL: She'd... she... She'd be ten now.
JOANIE: Good. What's she like?

(DARRYL *relapses. Radio noise cuts out. Silence. He doesn't answer.* JOANIE *takes his hand and firmly puts a stick of gum in his palm. She holds it tightly. Flickering subsides.*)

JOANIE: Peaches. That was my nickname as a kid – well, it was 'Strawberry and Peaches'. My Dad gave it to me. I couldn't wait until dinner – you know, those big old family dinners you always have – because, you know, I had the appetite of a seven-year-old girl. Girls have bigger appetites than boys at that age, I reckon.

(DARRYL *takes the stick of gum and puts in his mouth. He begins to chew.* JOANIE *chews a stick too.*)

My Dad would always sneak bubblegum from work for me and my brother; his office didn't have mints – they gave their employees bubblegum instead. Cheaper. He could only ever get the strawberry-fizz or peach-flavour sticks as those were the only ones left in the office at the end of the day. But we loved them. The fizz and pop. (*She pops a bubble.*) And that was my problem. I couldn't pick just the fizz or just the pop. It's not the same, right? You need both. They complement each other. So, I would lay the two sticks of strawberry and peach on top of each other – usually peach on the bottom so that I could roll the fizz up inside. And there you have a name. All rolled up in two perfect shades of pink. Named after unwanted confectionary. (*She chews a moment.*) Mom got out in '68. Got out of the house... out out out. (*With distaste:*) Carrie – I mean, Mom – got restless of our bubblegum lives, and Dad got fucked over. By her. The last thing he said to me? 'See you Peaches.' He moved to Michigan soon after that. Scott was old enough to take care of me by then. Dad gave us the house and everything – he did it properly. He didn't just leave, you know? He didn't completely abandon me. Scott says he found a new wife, a new life, and got himself some new kids, too. Who were we to stop him, right? It's his life now. But I like to think he went looking for Mom out west, and he never came back because he's still searching for her. (*Pause.*) Corny, I know, but there's a place for corny in the world right now, don't you think? Now I only ever chew peach, and it's all pop – all pop but no fizz.

SCENE SIX

(DARRYL *looks at her. Calmer, but still recovering.*)

DARRYL: She... She was about to get braces. Her mom wanted her to have perfect teeth. But... I thought she had the best smile in the world.

(*He begins to breathe slower. They still lock eyes. Pause. He pulls himself up.*)

JOANIE: And nobody calls me Peaches no more.

(*Silence. She smiles. He smiles back.*)

Not much talking goes on in the Black Hills, does it?
DARRYL (*recovering*): Get a few regulars that come through every coupla months. Folks don't stick around here. The horizon, there's too much of it in sight, too much to stand in front of. People don't like that. Being swallowed up by the land like that.
JOANIE: I guess we all like to feel important.

(JOANIE *suddenly reaches for the cola and swigs the bottle half dry with gusto. She wipes her mouth.*)

DARRYL: You two talk about change. But it's either moving too slowly or too quickly. It's dead out there. You must know that, don't you?

(CARRIE *gets up again to dance.* SCOTT *tries to take the glass from her. She pushes him away.*)

Look, the time of sipping on milkshakes and driving Cadillacs is over. So what comes next? Answer me that.

(*Pause.* SCOTT *tries to take the glass from* CARRIE, *but she pushes him away. He watches her.*)

CARRIE (*to herself*): We love too hard to hide the hole in our hearts.
DARRYL: With all you young people talking about Love up all the time, you'd think a whole lot more would be different.

(JOANIE *is silent.*)

Love is what is being dropped out of the planes, *love* is what steals, cheats, cracks and burns…

(*Radio air waves begin to ring again.*)

Love is what kills the strong… saves the… And they sent us into the… the… (*He begins to tremble.*)
JOANIE: We think we know how to love, but we don't. You… You were there, weren't you?

(*The lights flicker.*)

Darryl?

(*White. Blue. Lights come back on.* DARRYL *stops himself shaking. Long pause.*)

SCENE SIX

Hey, hey, that's better. I thought I lost you then.

(*The ringing stops.*)

You never know – the world may surprise you at how much it's learnt since Cadillacs and milkshakes.
DARRYL: That's something she'd say.
JOANIE: You said… back there… you have a little girl?
DARRYL: Yep.
JOANIE: How come you're with her now?
DARRYL: Got outta there, didn't I? Came back for Christmas.

(*Pause.*)

JOANIE: So, where is she, then?

(DARRYL *smiles.*)

SCENE SEVEN

CARRIE *collapses from dancing and struggles to lift herself up on to the bar.* SCOTT *lifts her by the waist and helps her on to it. She smiles. She sits on the bar and crosses her legs, panting. The light reveals clearly a large scarlet and blue bruise under her eye.*

CARRIE: Oh, wasn't that fun! Takes me right back! Why is it… that when you do… any strenuous exercise… you're always… gasping… afterwards for a… cigarette?

(*She reaches for* DARRYL*'s pack of cigarettes and lighter, takes one and lights up. She inhales and exhales with glee. Pause.*)

Do I remind you of Brigitte Bardot, Scottie? I don't mean to sound weird, but wouldn't you love to be around someone like that? Your mom's not real. She's a nark. You say that, right?
SCOTT (*flatly*): You missed a spot.
CARRIE: What?
SCOTT: Your… make-up. You missed… a little…

SCENE SEVEN

(SCOTT *takes her cigarette and puts it out. He points to her eye. She strokes it gingerly.* DARRYL *tries to turn away from* JOANIE. *She takes his hand in hers and holds it tightly.* CARRIE *grimaces.*)

There.
CARRIE: Oh... damn... Would you?
SCOTT: You'll be ready in time for beginners.

(SCOTT *rummages for powder, brush and blush amongst the remaining debris. He begins to apply the make-up to* CARRIE *softly.*)

CARRIE: Dream on – thinking she's more than what she is. Your father thought I was mysterious once.

(*Pause.*)

When I was a little girl, all I ever wanted to do was ride my bike everywhere and anywhere, usually around the same block of our neighbourhood every night. I had these handlebars with these glitter silver streamers, but, BUT the best thing was the glitter would peel off under my fingernails, and the wind would pick it off and stroke it through my hair. Going down a hill in Michigan was like getting a silver wind of dust in my eyes. And then I'd come back, walk through the front door and I *was* Brigitte Bardot, all sparkling with it in my hair and brushing my face. Well, it was either the glitter or the sweat from my going up the hills in the first place. I never thought of that before.
SCOTT: Makes a difference from another one of those 'in the wings' stories.

CARRIE: Yeah, you kids changed everything. No more green rooms after you two! (CARRIE *giggles.*) You start swallowing down the girl on the bike with the wind in her hair and the wishes in her heart. You swallow her down deep in your gut until the acid eats her up, like being trapped in the belly of a whale. Digested by this monster from the depths till there's nothing left. And I wasn't Carrie *Darling* any more. I was Caroline. Caroline. *Caroline.* Caroline who wears a helmet and doesn't eat cake on the grass, but bakes it and watches everyone else eat it.

SCOTT: There.

(SCOTT *finishes her make-up.*)

DARRYL (*struggling, quietly*): I'm not—
SCOTT: Perfect.
JOANIE } I'm here.
SCOTT

(*Pause.*)

CARRIE: Scott, please don't be scared. No one is completely good. If you try to be all the time, You'll explode one day.

SCENE EIGHT

JOANIE: You ran, didn't you?

(DARRYL *lets go of her hand. He moves away from her to the upstage door. He leans in the frame, looking out.*)

DARRYL: It's more than that.
JOANIE: I'm not judging.
DARRYL: That's exactly what people say when they do. And I didn't run away – you can be sure of that. Done with being twisted up tight by words. Ruth don't need me in her life right now.
JOANIE: I think we're all at our worst right now.
DARRYL: Perhaps. But I did *not* run away. Two separate things. They still think I'm out there. Came back for the holidays and everything, got in a car, got to our street, even got to the front door... but I couldn't do it.
JOANIE: You should go back.
DARRYL: You should go back.
JOANIE: She must miss you.
DARRYL: She was my girl, all right.

JOANIE: I mean Ruth. Your daughter. She must miss you.
DARRYL: I know. I know she does. Of course she does. Hell, I wish I could go back.
JOANIE: Then why don't you? What's stopping you?
DARRYL: It's complicated.
JOANIE: Urgh! Why is everyone saying that? It's lazy. The war? It's complicated. The students? It's complicated. The riots? It's complicated. The election? It's complicated. The president? It's complicated. The price of goddamn Oreos? It's complicated! Even Ruth is complicated.
DARRYL: She's just a little girl.
JOANIE: It's really very simple.
DARRYL: You're running away from it just like everyone else.
JOANIE: And you ran out on Ruth, not the goddamn country or war. Her.
DARRYL: I'll go back.
JOANIE: I don't think little Ruth will ever see her daddy again. She doesn't need you. And she doesn't need you to grow up, or fall in love, or to live her life.

(*Long pause.*)

DARRYL: You're all right.
JOANIE: I just don't understand why—
DARRYL: I know I left them, but it doesn't mean I'm gone, that I'm a ghost – I still love them, you know? Just cos I'm not there doesn't mean I don't care.
JOANIE: She could be out there now, thinking you're dead.
DARRYL: Plenty are. I'm not… I'm not good… inside.
JOANIE: She'll love you.

SCENE EIGHT

DARRYL: Would you want to see your daddy like that, back there?

(*Pause.*)

Would you still love him if he came home a monster?
JOANIE: I'd have to.
DARRYL: I couldn't. Her mom'll take care of her.
JOANIE: Don't be so sure about that. Moms get too much good press for what it's worth. So you gave birth to me? Well done. Anyone can do that.
DARRYL: You're not sweet at all, are you?
JOANIE: As apple fucking pie. You know anyone that truly is sweet?

(*Pause.*)

DARRYL: Hmmm… Jackie Kennedy?

(*They laugh.*)

Nah, I reckon she's a tiger behind the camera.
JOANIE: Well, she kept a clean house, I'll give her that. And that's not much.
DARRYL: Who else, then?
JOANIE: Scott.
DARRYL: Yeah, you've got your own regular Kennedy there.
JOANIE: I've got something there.

(*Pause.*)

He's almost too sweet, though. Poor guy.

DARRYL: Don't beat him up too much – you've gotta look after each other. Family, and all that.

(JOANIE *remembers* SCOTT. SCOTT *picks up* The Feminine Mystique *from the floor and flicks through its pages.*)

JOANIE: Can you do something for me?
DARRYL: Uh, sure, I guess.
JOANIE: Tell Scott... (*Takes the letter from her pocket.*) I've been carrying this around for ages... But... um... he can have it now. I... don't need it.
DARRYL: Hey now...

(JOANIE *joins* DARRYL *in the door frame upstage. Pause.*)

You, uh, got a dollar for that?

(*Pause.*)

You can owe me one some time.
JOANIE: Thanks.

(DARRYL *moves to take the pack of cigarettes and lighter from the bar.*)

Can I bum one?
DARRYL: Sure.
JOANIE: For the road.

(*She takes a cigarette. They exchange a look of understanding* JOANIE *takes the lighter and lights her cigarette, passing the lighter back to* DARRYL.)

SCENE NINE

SCOTT (*brandishing the book*): Mind if I give it a read?
CARRIE: Not at all.
SCOTT: Cool. Best not let Dad see you with it.
CARRIE: Taking care of me as always.

(SCOTT *laughs.* CARRIE *does so too, nervously. She takes the book from* SCOTT *and looks through it.*)

SCOTT: All of what you just said... Do you... do you – you don't have to answer if you don't want to, but – do... you... Do you wish you hadn't had me and Joanie?
CARRIE: Scottie, of course I don't! You're my children! Of course I don't – I just sometimes... I think... How could you ask me something like that? Your father has sacrificed... a lot for this family... and we love you both... very, very much. We were so young, so so young, when we had you. I was twenty-two... and I loved the world.

(JOANIE *exits the space through the upstage door leaving* DARRYL *alone.*)

I loved you most of all.

(*Pause.*)

SCOTT: Are you OK?
CARRIE: Oh yeah... just... Never mind.
SCOTT: Where did she go?
DARRYL: Joanie? Didn't say.
SCOTT: What did she say exactly?

(*Pause.* DARRYL *points to the letter.* SCOTT *reads it to himself.* SCOTT *looks at* DARRYL, *then the door, and then back at* DARRYL. CARRIE *finds a compact mirror. She looks under her eye. She winces. A burst of laughter erupts from* SCOTT, *disturbingly hysterical.*)

SCOTT: You play anything, Darryl?
DARRYL: Sure, I guess – blackjack, bit of poker—
SCOTT: No no no, an instrument. You play anything?
DARRYL: No not really, no. Not good enough, anyway.
SCOTT: Shame. Took you for a guitar-playin' kinda drunk.
DARRYL: Nope, just a straight-up drunk on a good day.

(JOANIE *enters the space again. She returns to the upstage door frame.* DARRYL *sees her.* SCOTT *continues, not seeing her.*)

Why?
SCOTT: 'Play me something, Scott. Play me something Dad would've liked,' she'd say. Dad always said it was the musical instrument of the greats: Mark Twain, Albert Einstein, Thomas Edison, Alexander Bell, Richard Nixon. Urgh. (*Pause.*) Nixon just made me lose this. Fuck. (*Finds his train of thought once more.*) I played for my school, for the kids in my class, for girls, sure. It

was middle school and girls always want a guy to play something for them. Not as sexy as the guitar, but hey, I made it work. Our family piano. A real Rockwell painting.

(CARRIE *feels her ribs. She winces harder. She looks under her clothes at further bruises. She looks back into the compact mirror.*)

Mom... Me... Joanie... and... and... and Dad.
CARRIE: I can't remember.

(*Pause.*)

SCOTT (*to* CARRIE): Come on, star, Dad'll be home soon. Put some smiles on to go with your new face and you'll make him happy.
CARRIE: But I'm not happy.

(*A spasm of pain hits her.* SCOTT *rushes to her. She recoils from him. Silence.*)

SCOTT: It didn't matter, those keys and these fingers, they were good together. But it never quite drowned out Dad coming back at night to Mom. Still got it all up here, though. I don't forget. The sound. The world just gets a whole lot more beautiful when you have someone to take care of, don't it? '71 I sold it. Got clear rid of it. Kicked it out when it was down on the G sharp one day.

(CARRIE *pets her bruises.*)

I found Mom the next morning slapped up in the door frame like a noosed-up schoolgirl. Her neck all busted up, back burnt up like summer plums bubbling under her skin. Piano didn't drown that out no more, the sound, that sound. Her howling for the man she loved to come back, and me praying that he didn't. That he wasn't the man doing that to her – that it was a stranger, not him. All I could do was just watch him chewing on his strawberry bubblegum like the homecoming king; mom's teeth his crown, and her head to toe in blue. All that was missing was something new. And Joanie, Daddy's little girl, asleep next door. And when the king retired, I showed her what I got for the piano. A 1968 Garrard 55B. I sold the piano and bought a record player. It didn't roar, it screamed. It screamed for her. Screaming like she did. The next day, we sat on the floor of the kitchen and listened to everything we had from before…

(A 1950s love song, such as 'The Wonder of You' by Ronnie Hilton, plays. CARRIE *remembers. She tries to dance again, but it hurts too much. White. Blue. White. Red. White.)*

Joanie didn't even stir in the next room. She didn't even stir. Just kept on dreaming. He'd put a stick of his gum under her pillow. Still dreaming, little Joanie. You see, we kept him busy enough so he wouldn't go into the next room. Joanie wishes I kept the piano. I don't. Mom used to, but she stopped wishing that pretty quickly. Because it drowned me out when it was my turn.

SCENE NINE

(*'The Wonder of You' fades.* SCOTT *watches* CARRIE. *He steadies her.*)

SCOTT: So... go.
CARRIE: What?
SCOTT: You... you could... just go. (*Pause.*) You could pack a bag. Get your coat. And leave.
CARRIE: And what do you want me to say? That I want to leave? That I don't love you? Would that make it easier?

(*Pause.*)

I'm not going.
SCOTT: You see... It was me.
DARRYL: How? It wasn't you.
SCOTT: It... was.
DARRYL: That was him, not you, kid.
SCOTT: But... I'm the one... who told her to leave.
DARRYL: I... Why didn't she take you with her?
CARRIE: I'm not leaving.
SCOTT: You have to.

(*Long Pause.*)

CARRIE: What about Joanie?

(*Pause.*)

SCOTT: I'll take care of her.
CARRIE: And who will take care of you?
SCOTT: I'm sure he will. In his own way.

CARRIE: Scott—
SCOTT: DON'T. Look. Dad'll be back within the hour. I don't pick up my bike. I walk and meet Joanie at school after her softball practice. I walk her home. You're not here. And a bag is missing. And we don't know where you are. (*Silence.*) I'm going now. She'll be waiting.
CARRIE: Scott. (*She stands, numb.*)
SCOTT: I gotta go.

(*White. Blue. Lights flicker.* SCOTT *leaves her.*)

CARRIE: SCOTT! I baked a pie for us all to have later after dinner! Make sure everyone gets a slice!

(*The radio tuning noise is heard.*)

SCOTT: I told her not to.

(*Pause.*)

And… She left.

(SCOTT *sees* JOANIE.)

JOANIE: Is that… is that… is all that true?
SCOTT: Joanie—
JOANIE: Tell me. NOW!

(CARRIE *rolls on to her side as if she has been kicked hard.*)

SCOTT: Yes.

SCENE NINE

(*Silence.*)

JOANIE: How?
SCOTT: You don't need to know.
JOANIE: Details.

(*Slight pause.*)

CARRIE (*cowering*): This is our little secret, baby.
JOANIE: Tell. Me. Now. I want to feel sick.
SCOTT: Hands… nails… heels… can lips… rings… knobs… forks… but… not… knives.
CARRIE: Why are you doing this? Make it stop!
SCOTT: Sometimes just her arm pressed into the dresser. It wasn't varnished. Splinters on the inside of her arm. On the inside of her thigh. That was the worst. Watching her use her tweezers to preen herself, sitting on the floor like she was picking out fleas. Each one pulled out with more and more gratification after the next. 'She needs it.' He'd say. 'She needs it.'
CARRIE: But… I love you.
SCOTT: We never wanted you to see her. Or me. Like that. I'm sorry.

(JOANIE *charges at* SCOTT. DARRYL *grabs her and restrains her. She tries to throw a punch but is buckled by* DARRYL. *She squirms in his arms. Lights flicker.* DARRYL *holds on to* JOANIE.)

CARRIE: Shh… Shh… Shh… darling, stop it. Stop it, sweetheart. He's not the one you want to hurt. Stop it. There, there. He's not the one. He's not the one. He loves you. He loves you. He loves you. Remember what that felt like?

(JOANIE *hangs in* DARRYL*'s arms, limp, exhausted. She tears herself away from him. She snatches the letter from* SCOTT *and brandishes it at* DARRYL. *Shaking.*)

JOANIE: Read it.
CARRIE: I…
JOANIE: Go on. You have let me believe in this for thirteen years!

(JOANIE *forces it into* DARRYL*'s hand.*)

READ. IT.
CARRIE (*helplessly*): Joanie…
DARRYL (*reading out loud*): Dear Mommy and Daddy…

(*Lights flicker.* CARRIE *reaches for a bottle and takes a gulp. She coughs hard. On her hands and knees, she begins to pack what's left of the debris into* JOANIE*'s suitcase.*)

I know by now you must have found each other again. I wonder if you are somewhere sunny. I hope you are. I made pitcher this week and Scott has got his first car so I don't have to ride on the front of his bike any more! Which is good. We really miss you and Scott says we'll find you both one day, and we'll be a family again. And maybe we could get the piano back too?

(DARRYL *continues to read.*)

I miss you.

(CARRIE *finishes packing.*)

I love you Daddy. I love you Mommy.

(*White. Lights stop flickering.*)

CARRIE: Joanie, my little girl.

(*Silence. She splutters again, and leans against the case.*)

SCOTT: He did it. Dad did. Don't hate her any more. Don't hate this family any more. She didn't abandon us. She escaped.
JOANIE: AND YOU TOLD HER TO GO WITHOUT US! What a big fucking brother you are. Thank you so much for protecting me from the very bad men in the very bad world.
SCOTT: I was trying to be—
JOANIE: A king! You were trying to be a fucking king! When all I wanted was my brother.

(DARRYL *moves to the upstage door.*)

You're leaving?
DARRYL: Uhuh.
JOANIE: Ruth?

(DARRYL *nods.*)

Go to her. (*Points to the door.*)

SCOTT: What about our wheels?
JOANIE: He'll take them. (*To* DARRYL:) Right?
DARRYL: Yeah. Sure. I gotta get somewhere.
SCOTT: But Da—
DARRYL: You're on your own, Kennedy boy.
JOANIE: Go. Now. Ruth.

(DARRYL *exits.*)

(*Turning:*) How many times?
SCOTT: I don't know.
JOANIE: Come on, I'm a big girl now. Was he more of a 'when I'm in the mood' type, the 'after a few Scotches' type, the 'first Wednesday of every month' type? Come on!
SCOTT: There wasn't a pattern, if that's what you mean.
JOANIE: More.
SCOTT: 'She needs it,' he'd say. 'She needs it.' She needed me. Her son.
JOANIE: You and her. You and her all the way.
SCOTT: It wasn't supposed to be like that.
JOANIE: There was too much of him in me for her to love me, wasn't there?
SCOTT: We were protecting you.
JOANIE: And who was protecting her? What did I do wrong that you two didn't need me—
SCOTT: What did I do?
JOANIE: What did I do wrong? She needed it? She fucking needed it?
CARRIE: I needed it.

SCENE NINE

(JOANIE *slaps herself. Red.* SCOTT *tries to stop her. She pushes him off and runs away from him.* CARRIE *drags the suitcase with effort, crawling, to the upstage door.*)

JOANIE: She needed it. (*Slaps herself.*) She needed it.

(*Blue.*)

Tell me what he did. Tell me what she never could. Now!

(CARRIE *reaches the door with the case. She drags it against the frame.* JOANIE *slaps herself furiously in a blindness.*)

SCOTT: Joanie, you've got to stop!
CARRIE: You've got to stop! Listen to me. Listen to me!

(JOANIE *grabs* SCOTT *hard.*)

JOANIE: I want to know what it felt like. Hit me like he did, Scott. Hit me now!

(*White. Blue.*)

SCOTT: No! Stop it! Stop it! Stop it!

(SCOTT *shakes* JOANIE *hard.*)

JOANIE: I. NEED. IT.
CARRIE: NO. MORE.

(SCOTT *is motionless, holding* JOANIE *rooted.*)

SCOTT: I need you to stop. I love you, Joanie. I'm not going to do this... He was wrong. I promise you, he was wrong.

JOANIE: That's what he said to her – he told her he loved her so much before it. Before... before... before...

CARRIE: Before... before... before...

JOANIE: Us. Scott. Did Mommy smell of dried blood? Did she wear red like a soldier in battle?

CARRIE: I love you so much, darling girl.

(JOANIE *slaps herself. White.*)

JOANIE: I won't stop until you stop it. Because I fucking need it. Hit me!

(*Pause.*)

For God's sake, hit me!

(*Pause.*)

SCOTT: I won't!
CARRIE: I can't!
SCOTT: I don't want to!
CARRIE: Dreams! Nothing but dreams!

(JOANIE *hits* SCOTT *hard. Radio tuning noise sounds again, louder than before. Red.* SCOTT *spits hard. White. Blue. Darkness. 'Chirpy Chirpy Cheep Cheep' echoes. Pause. Lights up.* CARRIE *is gone.* SCOTT *and* JOANIE *are alone. They lock on to one another.*)

SCENE NINE

SCOTT: There's the old man in the girl yet. And he did it much harder than that.

(*The echo continues.* JOANIE *backhands* SCOTT *on the other side.* SCOTT *shifts his heels slightly. He spits on the other side.*)

Closer.

(*She hits him harder. Blue. Echoes.*)

Closer.

(*She hits him harder. Red.*)

Still love you, sister. And I'm not going anywhere.

(*Echoes. Slight pause. She right-hooks* SCOTT *hard. White. Red. He staggers to the ground.* JOANIE *pants. She stands over him.*)

And then he'd say, 'I love you.'

(*Pause.* JOANIE *kicks* SCOTT. *Bright white. They collapse and fall down next to each other. Panting hard together. Silence.*)

JOANIE: So… that's where… I get the best arm… in the family from. I made pitcher, too. I remember him… being so fucking proud.

(*Long pause.*)

SCOTT: Shame about the brains.

JOANIE: All right, pretty boy.
SCOTT: I am not a boy.
JOANIE: You ain't pretty any more, either.
SCOTT: Yeah.
JOANIE: Mama's boy.
SCOTT: Daddy's girl.

(*Pause.*)

JOANIE: Didn't you borrow my eyeliner last February?
SCOTT: That was for a concert.
JOANIE: I want it back.
SCOTT: You're bringing this up now?
JOANIE: I never got it back. It's mine.
SCOTT: Well, you have to admit, I do look better in eyeliner than you.
JOANIE: Yeah, you're a real pro with ladies' make-up, big brother.
SCOTT: Sure am. And much better at it than you.
JOANIE: Scott?
SCOTT: Hmm?
JOANIE: Who was that phone call to?

(*Pause.*)

SCOTT: What?
JOANIE: Who did you call? Out back?
SCOTT: I…
JOANIE: Who was it, Scott?

(*Long pause.*)

SCENE NINE

Don't.

(JOANIE *gets up and moves to the upstage door to exit. She stops. Pause.*)

They're waiting for us out there.

(SCOTT *staggers to his feet.*)

SCOTT: I said I'm not going… to let you go… out there… alone.
JOANIE: I know… So… stop… me.

(*Radio tuning increases to a crescendo. Darkness.*)

THE END

ACKNOWLEDGEMENTS

Special thanks go to the drama department at Centre College, Kentucky, and to the Norton Centre for the Arts, for the very first inkling of an idea, where the first scene of this play was presented under a different name.

To the Soho Writers Lab and all of my cohort for the guidance, trust and confidence given to me – especially when I changed my entire play idea halfway through to *Black Hills*! To Anthony Lau for mentoring me while I was writing this play at the Soho Theatre, and for believing in these characters and their world.

To Frank Lanza for his talent in finding friendship, adventure and the perfect shot with your camera in America. Your photography and continued friendship contributed to the world and feeling of this America. Keep driving.

To my publisher, Will Dady, for your continued and dedicated approach to each play, each of which has its own identity to the last, and your careful handling of each one. Your guidance and trust shines through your hard work at Renard Press.

ABOUT THE AUTHOR

EMMA ZADOW is an actor, playwright and screenwriter from Norfolk. She trained at Rose Bruford College as an actor, and her plays have been performed at the Arcola, the Old Red Lion Theatre, The King's Head, Camden Fringe Festival, Norwich Arts Centre and Pleasance Theatre. Emma is an alumni playwright from the Soho Theatre Writers Lab, a Last Conker Screenwriter Mentee and Mercury Theatre Playwright 2022, and she was shortlisted for the ETPEP Award and Tony Craze Award. A BBC New Creative, her screenplays include the hit short film *The Cromer Special* and the BBC short *Jigging*, which won Best Experimental Short at the Hollywood Boulevard Film Festival and was Semi-Finalist at the San Francisco Arthouse Festival.

EMMAZADOW.COM 🌐 🐦 @EMMAZADOW

WWW.RENARDPRESS.COM

ALSO BY EMMA ZADOW:

FRIDGE

Alice hasn't been home for a while – for seven years, in fact. But when her little sister Lo tries to take her own life, she has to return to the life she left behind. The change of scenery from London to Norfolk proves quite the culture shock, however, and Alice has to confront what she left behind all those years ago.

The sisters' relationship hasn't evolved in Alice's absence, and when she steps through the door she's plunged back into the same world she escaped from. Set against Norfolk's bleak landscapes, but masquerading as childhood nostalgia, *Fridge* is an all-too-familiar exploration of the broken promises of youth, and a bitter exposition of a generation left behind.

ISBN: 9781913724238 • 96pp • £10

ALSO BY EMMA ZADOW:

IN THE MOSS

Exponentially increasing levels of unemployment and simmering racial tension in Moss Side, inner Manchester, exploded into mass riots on the 8th of July 1981, following the siege of a police station.

In the Moss frames the events from the perspectives of Janet, a student nurse working in A&E, and Nav, a Sikh police officer on the streets. Both crave a return to normality and just want to fit in, but when violence breaks out and a teenage boy is stabbed, they are thrust together and forced to confront questions that arise about what really happened in the Moss.

ISBN: 9781913724559 • 96pp • £10

MORE PLAYSCRIPTS FROM RENARD PRESS

ISBN: 9781913724238
96pp • Paperback • £10

ISBN: 9781913724559
96pp • Paperback • £10

ISBN: 9781913724962
80pp • Paperback • £7.99

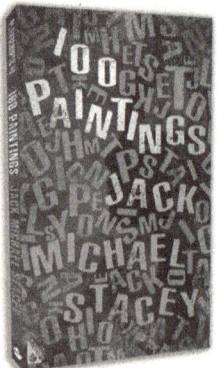

ISBN: 9781804470121
80pp • Paperback • £7.99

ISBN: 9781804470145
72pp • Paperback • £7.99

DISCOVER THE FULL COLLECTION AT WWW.RENARDPRESS.COM